# PJ's Christmas Key

**Written by Jerry Yarnell**

Illustrated by Hazel Mitchell

© 2008 Jerry Yarnell

Published by:
Zoë Life Publishing
P.O. Box 871066
Canton, MI 48187 USA
www.zoelifepub.com

All rights reserved. No part of this book may be reproduced or transmitted in any form or by any means including, but not limited to, electronic or mechanical, photocopying, recording, or by any information storage and retrieval system without written permission from the publisher, except for the inclusion of brief quotations in review.

Author:         Jerry Yarnell
Illustrator:    Hazel Mitchell
Editor:         Jessica Colvin

First U.S. Edition 2008

Publisher's Cataloging-in-Publication Data

Yarnell, Jerry.

PJ's Christmas key / Jerry Yarnell ; illustrated by Hazel Mitchell.

p. cm.

ISBN 978-1-934363-48-5

1. Christmas—Juvenile fiction. 2. Jesus Christ—Juvenile fiction. 3. God—Omniscience. 4. Pennsylvania—Fiction.

PZ7.Y198 2009
813`.3 —dc22        2008938489

Summary: PJ learns the real key to Christmas and all its treasures is Jesus.

10 Digit ISBN 1-934363-48-0 Perfect bound softcover
13 Digit ISBN 978-1-934363-48-5 Perfect bound softcover

For current information about releases by Jerry Yarnell or other releases from Zoë Life Publishing, visit our web site: http://www.zoelifepub.com

Printed in the United States of America

# v3.1 12 03 08

# Dedication

To my daughter, Stephanie Lee

# Acknowledgements

The problem with acknowledgements is the danger of leaving someone out. I would like to thank all who have been part of my journey of faith in the Lord. First and foremost is my Savior, Lord, and friend, Jesus. There have been countless Sunday school teachers as well as mentors and brothers and sisters in Christ and I am grateful to them.

I need to thank my best friend—my wife Pam, who has weathered many a storm with me as we have tried to serve our Lord. Thanks to my parish for giving me time to try my hand at Christian writing. I thank as well my co-pastor, the Rev. Drex Morton, a true brother in the Lord. Thank you to my daughter Stephanie for her help in typing as well as Walley and Shirley Smith who were great benefactors in this work.

Last but not least, the family of Zoë Life Publishing, Sabrina Adams, Founder, CEO and Publisher, Julie Grannis, client services, Jessica Colvin, editor and Hazel Mitchell, illustrator.

In all may the Lord be glorified.

*Pastor Jerry Yarnell*

# PJ's Christmas Key

**Written by Jerry Yarnell**

Illustrated by Hazel Mitchell

# FOREWORD

Hi! My name is Phinehas Josiah Stanley. It's a real mouthful, isn't it? My name has been in my family since Biblical times. A long time ago, even before my grandfather was born, our family's last name was **Shamayim**. I heard one of the grownups say it meant **heaven** in Hebrew. But it was so hard to say and spell that one day they changed it to Stanley, go figure.

I was named after two people in the Bible: Phinehas was a great leader and high priest during the time when Moses was leading the people of God to the Promised Land. Josiah was a king of Judah who led the people back to God when they had been worshiping false gods. Phinehas Josiah is hard to say, so everyone just calls me PJ.

I live in a little town in the mountains of Pennsylvania. Our valley was first called Nittany Valley, but now it is also known as Happy Valley. The town is surrounded by beautiful countryside with farms, forests, and streams. My family lives in the middle of town close to the school. It's just my mom and dad, me, my older brother Richard and my younger sister Patty.

On the outskirts of town, near the forest, my grandparents live on a farm. We call my grandfather Grandpap. Grandpap and Grandma are the best grandparents anyone could ever have. They love to play all types of games Sometimes they even take us on the most exciting adventures. They are always thoughtful and get us the neatest things—which brings us to this story!

One bright, sunny winter morning, PJ Stanley woke up to the most wonderful smell of his mother's French toast and sausage.

She made the best French toast in the whole world! It was so gooey and delicious.

PJ rushed downstairs to fill his tummy.

"Okay kids, after breakfast we need to get the nativity out and put it on the mantle," Mrs. Stanley said.

It was just five days before Christmas, and the whole house was decorated with beautiful ornaments, bows, ribbons, and lights. PJ, Richard, and Patty gobbled up their delicious French toast.

Suddenly, the doorbell rang. "Ding dong!" It was the mailman. He had a large box, a special delivery addressed to the whole Stanley family.

"Looks like Grandma and Grandpap sent us some Christmas presents," Mrs. Stanley said. "They are on vacation and won't be able to spend Christmas day with us."

"Well it sure was nice of them to send us presents, wasn't it kids?" their father said while opening the big box. "Let's get these out and put them under the tree."

PJ noticed right away that there were two gifts for

him. He felt the gifts and shook them. One was a book, he could tell by the feel of it. He wasn't sure about the other one. As PJ shook it, he heard that there was something inside. He was certain he knew what was in the box. It had to be the number one gift on his list: a remote control monster truck that could climb over things.

PJ was sure the truck was in there. At Thanksgiving dinner, his grandparents had asked him what he wanted for Christmas. He told them about the truck, gave them its name, and even told them what store they could find it in. The present they sent was a different shaped box than the one PJ had seen in the store. Still, he was sure the truck he wanted was in that gift.

PJ!" his mother warned. "No touching the presents till Christmas!"

"Okay," PJ replied. But he had to check out the other present that felt like a book. There was a strange note attached. He quickly read it. It said, "Open and read me first!"

PJ listened to his mother and left the presents alone, but he didn't know what to make of the note.

The week was longer than any other week in PJ's life. He thought Christmas would never come!

He helped his mom put up the nativity scene…

He decorated Christmas cookies with his sister…

And he had fun outside in the snow…

But still, the time wasn't passing fast enough.

Then, just when PJ thought he couldn't wait any longer, he woke up and realized the big day had finally arrived.

"Woo hoo! Get up! Get up everybody!" PJ shouted, running up and down the hallway. "It's Christmas! It's Christmas! Woooo hoooo!"

Richard and Patty came racing out of their bedrooms.

All three children clamored down the stairs and sat around the tree. When Mr. and Mrs. Stanley came downstairs, and everyone was seated, they were allowed to start opening presents. "Okay kids, go ahead," their father said.

PJ reached for the box he thought contained his truck, but his mother stopped him. "Sweetie," she said, "didn't you see the note? Open the other one first."

PJ knew he had no choice, so he ripped open the first gift. It was a book. Its title was "The Key to Christmas." It was a story about the birth of Jesus.

PJ knew the story from Sunday school and church, so he just pretended to read the book. No one was looking, so he closed the book and said, "Okay, I'm done." He had not read it, but he thought no one would know.

PJ tore open the second gift. Inside was a wooden treasure chest that his Grandfather had made for him. It had a rounded top with his initials PJS painted on it. It was beautiful and PJ wanted to open it. From shaking the gift he could tell something was inside because it moved back and forth. He just knew it was the truck he wanted.

When he tried to open the treasure chest, he found it was locked. He needed a key. PJ looked all around for the key, but couldn't find it. His Grandparents had forgotten to send it! He couldn't get to what he was sure was his remote controlled monster truck.

After looking for the key, PJ went on to open his other gifts. They were wonderful with many gifts of clothes and toys—but no truck. After all the gifts were open, PJ looked again and again for the key to his treasure chest, but couldn't find it.

Suddenly, PJ's brother had an idea. "What if we call Grandma and Grandpap? We could wish them a Merry Christmas," Richard said. "And we could ask them where PJ's treasure chest key is!"

"They're not at home, kids," Mrs. Stanley said. "Remember? They're on vacation. They won't be home until late tonight."

It was a long day. PJ played with his other toys and gifts, but he kept coming back to the treasure chest. He tried again and again to open the chest, but it wouldn't budge.

When the phone rang later that evening, PJ ran to answer it. He was polite enough to wish his grandparents a Merry Christmas, but then said quickly, "You forgot to send the key to the treasure chest!"

"No," Grandpap chuckled. "We sent it. You must not have followed our instructions. Did you read the book we sent you?"

"Well, no," PJ replied. "I was going to read it later."

PJ's Grandfather said, "You know we love you PJ. God

loves you too. God gives us instructions in the Bible so He can bless us. If we can't follow his Word then we miss the blessings He has for us. God tells us, "If you will obey my voice and keep my commandments then you shall be my people" (Exod. 19:5). In other words, God's blessings have a condition attached. God loves everyone, but many miss His blessings by not following His instructions. Follow our instructions carefully and you will find the key to your treasure chest. Just as the birth of Christ is the key to life and life's joy! God really desires for you to be happy. That will only truly happen when we follow and obey Jesus."

"Okay…thanks Grandpap," PJ said. Then he handed the phone over to his parents.

He picked up the book, The Key to Christmas, and carefully read the story of God's love coming to the world at Christmas. It was the story of Jesus' birth. The birth of Jesus at Christmas is the key to our salvation! PJ read every single word, and when he turned to the very last page of the book, there was a shiny key taped to the paper. A note was also written on the page that read, "PJ, remember the key to Christmas and all its treasures! Love, Grandma and Grandpap."

PJ gently took the key off the page and ran to his treasure chest. It easily opened the lock and inside was the monster truck he had wanted. As he took out the truck, there was another note. It read "PJ, God loves you! He sent Jesus into the world on Christmas to save you. God wants to bless you with many treasures. Listen to Him. We love you, Grandma and Grandpap."

Then he started up his truck and had it climb over the pile of gifts under their Christmas tree. As he did, he smiled and whispered, "Oh, and Lord, don't forget to bless my Grandma and Grandpap…"

## About the Author

Jerry Yarnell is a fun-loving man of faith. He loves to laugh and tell stories to people young and old. He has been blessed with a loving wife, Pamela, who offers devoted friendship and joy. They were married in 1971 and have a beautiful daughter, Stephanie.

After earning his bachelor's degree in 1972 at Rutgers University, he attended Gettysburg Theological Seminary for his Masters in Divinity. Then, in 1981 he became a Doctor of Ministry after graduating from the Lutheran School of Theology at Chicago.

Jerry currently serves as Senior Pastor at St. Michael Lutheran Church in Canton, Michigan where he has been for the last thirty years. Previously, for two years, he served as Associate Pastor for Bethlehem Lutheran Church in Traverse City, Michigan.

In addition to his work as a pastor and author, Jerry loves being outdoors hunting and fishing. He also enjoys the companionship of his golden retriever, Hannah, and his cockapoo, Buck.

To order additional copies of *PJ's Christmas Key* or to find out about other books by Jerry Yarnell or Zoë Life Publishing, please visit our website www.zoelifepub.com.

Contact Outreach at Zoë Life Publishing:

Zoë Life Publishing
P.O. Box 871066
Canton, MI 48187
(877)841-3400
outreach@zoelifepub.com